SCIENTISTS AND THEIR DISCOVERIES
BENJAMIN FRANKLIN

SCIENTISTS AND THEIR DISCOVERIES

ALBERT EINSTEIN

ALEXANDER FLEMING

ALFRED NOBEL

BENJAMIN FRANKLIN

CHARLES DARWIN

GALILEO

GREGOR MENDEL

ISAAC NEWTON

LEONARDO DA VINCI

LOUIS PASTEUR

THOMAS EDISON

SCIENTISTS AND THEIR DISCOVERIES
BENJAMIN FRANKLIN

BRADLEY SNEDDON

MASON CREST

Mason Crest
450 Parkway Drive, Suite D
Broomall, Pennsylvania 19008
(866) MCP-BOOK (toll-free)
www.masoncrest.com

Printed and bound in the United States of America.

CPSIA Compliance Information: Batch #SG2018.
For further information, contact Mason Crest at 1-866-MCP-Book.

First printing
9 8 7 6 5 4 3 2 1

Library of Congress Cataloging-in-Publication Data on file with the Library of Congress

ISBN: 978-1-4222-4027-4 (hc)
ISBN: 978-1-4222-7759-1 (ebook)

Scientists and their Discoveries series ISBN: 978-1-4222-4023-6

Developed and Produced by National Highlights Inc.
Interior and cover design: Yolanda Van Cooten
Production: Michelle Luke

QR CODES AND LINKS TO THIRD-PARTY CONTENT
You may gain access to certain third-party content ("Third-Party Sites") by scanning and using the QR Codes that appear in this publication (the "QR Codes"). We do not operate or control in any respect any information, products, or services on such Third-Party Sites linked to by us via the QR Codes included in this publication, and we assume no responsibility for any materials you may access using the QR Codes. Your use of the QR Codes may be subject to terms, limitations, or restrictions set forth in the applicable terms of use or otherwise established by the owners of the Third-Party Sites. Our linking to such Third-Party Sites via the QR Codes does not imply an endorsement or sponsorship of such Third-Party Sites or the information, products, or services offered on or through the Third-Party Sites, nor does it imply an endorsement or sponsorship of this publication by the owners of such Third-Party Sites.

Publisher's Note: Websites listed in this book were active at the time of publication. The publisher is not responsible for websites that have changed their address or discontinued operation since the date of publication. The publisher reviews and updates the websites each time the book is reprinted.

CONTENTS

KEY ICONS TO LOOK FOR:

Words to understand: These words with their easy-to-understand definitions will increase the reader's understanding of the text while building vocabulary skills.

Sidebars: This boxed material within the main text allows readers to build knowledge, gain insights, explore possibilities, and broaden their perspectives by weaving together additional information to provide realistic and holistic perspectives.

Educational videos: Readers can view videos by scanning our QR codes, providing them with additional educational content to supplement the text. Examples include news coverage, moments in history, speeches, iconic sports moments, and much more!

Text-dependent questions: These questions send the reader back to the text for more careful attention to the evidence presented there.

Research projects: Readers are pointed toward areas of further inquiry connected to each chapter. Suggestions are provided for projects that encourage deeper research and analysis.

Series glossary of key terms: This back-of-the-book glossary contains terminology used throughout the series. Words found here increase the reader's ability to read and comprehend higher-level books and articles in this field.

View of the historic cemetery on Copp's Hill in Boston; in the background is the steeple of the Old North Church. Boston was founded in 1630, less than eighty years before the birth of Benjamin Franklin.

WORDS TO UNDERSTAND

almanac—a calendar of months and days, with information about astronomy and matters of general interest.

common-law marriage—a marriage in which the partners lives together for a period of time (generally at least seven years) and tells friends, family, and the community that they are married, but never go through a formal ceremony or get a marriage license.

surety—an item of value that is left to guarantee that a person will perform a duty, such as returning a borrowed book to the library.

CHAPTER 1

The Printer Who Became a Scientist

A highly successful forty-two-year-old businessman, who had earned a comfortable living as a printer and publisher, would seem unlikely to become one of the world's most influential scientists. But Benjamin Franklin did just that. Soon after his "retirement" from business, Franklin made discoveries that would prove vital to our present-day understanding of electricity and of physical substances. Moreover, within nine years of this astonishing change in his life, Franklin plunged into yet another world—politics. He set off for London to embark on a political crusade that would occupy him almost to the end of his life.

Benjamin Franklin was born in Boston, Massachusetts, on January 17, 1706. Boston was then a small but growing seaport. It was home to many immigrants from Europe, who had made the arduous sea crossing to North America in search of a better life. Benjamin's father, Josiah Franklin, was among them. In 1683 Josiah Franklin had sailed to Boston with his young wife, Anne, and their three children. He was a soap and candle maker from the Oxfordshire town of Banbury in England. Soon after arriving in America, he managed to establish a flourishing business. A few years later, Anne Franklin died and Josiah remarried. His second wife, Abiah Folger, was an American from Nantucket. Josiah had seventeen children from these marriages. Young Benjamin was the fifteenth.

Growing Up in Massachusetts

Josiah Franklin was very well educated, and taught Benjamin to read at an early age. He hoped that his son would one day become a minister in the Church of England. But when Benjamin had been at grammar school for a year, Josiah took him away from the school, perhaps because he could no longer afford it. Benjamin was sent to a man called Mr. Brownell, who taught him writing and arithmetic. Writing gave Benjamin few problems, but, as he said years later, "I failed in the arithmetic, and made no progress in it."

Soon Josiah needed help in running his business, so it made sense to him to halt Benjamin's education and to employ him as an assistant. Benjamin very soon made it quite clear that making soap and candles was not to his liking. Josiah was anxious to find Benjamin a job, so he took his restless young son on visits to various craftsmen around the town, to try and interest him in one of these trades. None of the crafts took Benjamin's fancy. His ambition was to become a sailor. One of his brothers had already run away to sea, but his father was determined that Benjamin should not do the same.

So, perhaps as a last resort, twelve-year-old Benjamin was apprenticed to his brother James, who was a printer. James was eight years older than Benjamin, and had learned the printing

Franklin would have used a hornbook like this one while studying at school in Boston. His formal education was limited to just one year.

YOUNG INVENTOR

Benjamin Franklin displayed his ingenuity even when he was a teenager. Like many children brought up near the sea, he was fond of boats and swimming. He wanted to find a way to swim more quickly, and so he made paddles, in the shape of an artist's palette, and attached them to his hands and feet. These certainly worked, but they made him tired very quickly. Franklin was unsatisfied with the performance of the paddles fixed to his feet, and much later in his life concluded that much of the thrust (he probably used a sort of "frog kick," as a modern breaststroke swimmer would) came from the insides of the feet and the ankles—which is why the foot paddles were less effective than he had hoped.

trade in London. James had just returned to Boston with his own press and was in the process of setting up a printing shop. This was the start of Benjamin's real education, though his father and brother could hardly have known so at the time. The boy's hours of work were long and the conditions laid down for his nine-year apprenticeship were, by modern standards, severe. Benjamin was delighted to be involved in writing and publishing, and the little spare time he had was spent in reading, learning languages and, later, in writing.

In 1721 James founded a newspaper called the *New-England Courant*. It was a daring venture, for the articles attacked well-known political and religious figures in the Boston area. Benjamin was impressed by this style of comment and wrote his own articles for the *Courant*, even though this was forbidden by the terms of his apprenticeship. He used the pen name "Silence Dogood" so that nobody would guess his real identity, and slipped the articles under the shop door at night.

THE
New-England Courant.

From MONDAY June 4. to MONDAY June 11. 1722.

Quem Dies videt veniens Superbum,
Hunc Dies vidit fugiens jacentem.

Seneca.

To the Author of the New-England Courant.

S I R, [No VI.

MONG the many reigning Vices of the Town which may at any Time come under my Confideration and Reprehenfion, there is none which I am more inclin'd to expofe than that of *Pride*. It is acknowledg'd by all to be a Vice the moft hateful to God and Man. Even thofe who nourifh it in themfelves, hate to fee it in others. The proud Man afpires after Nothing lefs than an unlimited Superiority over his Fellow-Creatures. He has made himfelf a King in *Soliloquy*; fancies himfelf conquering the World, and the Inhabitants thereof confulting on proper Methods to acknowledge his Merit. I fpeak it to my Shame, I my felf was a Queen from the Fourteenth to the Eighteenth Year of my Age, and govern'd the World all the Time of my being govern'd by my Mafter. But this fpeculative Pride may be the Subject of another Letter: I fhall at prefent confine my Thoughts to what we call *Pride of Apparel*. This Sort of Pride has been growing upon us ever fince we parted with our Homefpun Cloaths for *Fourteen Penny Stuff*, &c. And the *Pride of Apparel* has begot and nourifh'd in us a *Pride of Heart*, which portends the Ruin of Church and State. *Pride goeth before Deftruction, and a haughty Spirit before a Fall*: And I remember my late Reverend Husband would often fay upon this Text, That a Fall was the *natural Confequence*, as well as *Punifhment* of Pride. Daily Experience is fufficient to evince the Truth of this Obfervation. Perfons of fmall Fortune under the Dominion of this Vice, feldom confider their Inability to maintain themfelves in it, but ftrive to imitate their Superiors in Eftate, or Equals in Folly, until one Misfortune comes upon the Neck of another, and every Step they take is a Step backwards. By ftriving to appear rich they become really poor, and deprive themfelves of that Pity and Charity which is due to the humble poor Man, who is made fo more immediately by Providence.

THIS Pride of Apparel will appear the more foolifh, if we confider, that thofe airy Mortals, who have no other Way of making themfelves confiderable but by gorgeous Apparel, draw after them Crowds of Imitators, who hate each other while they endeavour after a Similitude of Manners.

Church, the Hall, or the Kitchen; and if a Number of them were well mounted on *Noddles-Ifland*, they would look more like Engines of War for bombarding the Town, than Ornaments of the Fair Sex. An honeft Neighbour of mine, happening to be in Town fome time fince on a publick Day, inform'd me, that he faw four Gentlewomen with their Hoops half mounted in a Balcony, as they withdrew to the Wall, to the great Terror of the Militia, who (he thinks) might attribute their irregular Volleys to the formidable Appearance of the Ladies Petticoats.

I ASSURE you, Sir, I have but little Hopes of perfwading my Sex, by this Letter, utterly to relinquifh the extravagant Foolery, and Indication of Immodefty, in this monftrous Garb of their's; but I would at leaft defire them to leffen the Circumference of their Hoops, and leave it with them to confider, Whether they, who pay no Rates or Taxes, ought to take up more Room in the King's High-Way, than the Men, who yearly contribute to the Support of the Government.

V

I am, Sir,
Your Humble Servant,
SILENCE DOGOOD.

—— *Fungar vice cotis.* —— Hor.

S I R,

I HOPE a Difcourfe of a ferious Nature, efpecially upon a Subject which deferves the utmoft attention of all that wifh well to Mankind, won't prove unacceptable to many of your Readers. And perhaps it won't fall under the view and confideration of more Perfons in any other way of Publication, than it will in your Paper, if you fhall pleafe to allow it a Place there. I doubt not of your readinefs to forward any thing to the view of the World, which you may apprehend likely to do good in it: and I believe every Man who hath *an enlarged Heart*, and *a generous defire* to be an *extenfive Bleffing*, will rejoice to have any Way of being fo fuggefted to him, from whatever Quarter the hint may happen to come.

IT is certainly the earneft Defire of every Good Man to be as great a Benefactor to Mankind as poffibly he can, and there is no Man that hath a due Senfe of the Bufinefs he was fent into the World about, but what laments it as his great unhappinefs, that his Capacity is not equal to his good Will to Men. And yet it is furprifing to Obferve, how ftrangely fome of the moft effectual Methods of doing a great deal of Good, are *overlook'd* by Men who have it in *the Power of their Hands to do it*, and it may be make it a confiderable part of their daily Care to *devife Liberal Things*.

I fhall mention but one Inftance at this Time, it

The authorities soon became displeased with the tone of James's newspaper. In 1722 he was sent to prison for a month, and Benjamin took charge. More and more often, Silence Dogood's opinions were published, and the attacks on the colonial authorities continued. In January 1723 the authorities decided that they would not tolerate any more of these articles, and James was forbidden to print or publish the paper. A devious scheme was worked out to allow Benjamin, though strictly still apprenticed to James, to carry on publishing the *Courant*, by publishing it under his name instead, with the articles toned down so that they would not be found quite so offensive.

Finding His Own Way

By September of 1723, Benjamin's writing skills and his personality had developed so much that he was no longer content to serve his brother. Though he felt very guilty about breaking their agreement, Benjamin fled from Boston and arrived in New York three days later. He found no work in New York and moved on to Philadelphia. He arrived tired and hungry, and spent his last few coins on three loaves of bread. As he wandered along the street clutching his bread, he later recalled that a pretty woman standing in a doorway laughed at him.

Scan here to watch a short video about the founding of Pennsylvania and other "middle colonies."

Drawing of Philadelphia as it appeared in the 1720s, when Benjamin Franklin arrived from Boston.

Benjamin's fortunes soon improved. He found work, made a good name for himself, and in 1725 ventured to London for a year—the first of several trips he was to make across the Atlantic. He returned when an old friend offered him work in Philadelphia. By 1730 he owned his own business.

In September 1730, Deborah Read—the woman who had laughed at him seven years earlier, became his wife. Theirs was a **common-law marriage**. Franklin had courted Deborah before he first sailed to London five years earlier, but after he left, she had married another man. Her husband vanished on a trip to the West Indies, and it was rumored that he had died there. However, because there was no proof of his death, Franklin's marriage to Deborah could not be officially consecrated in a church. Despite this, their partnership lasted forty-five years. Franklin and Deborah had two children: Francis (who died in childhood) and Sarah. Deborah also helped Franklin raise his illegitimate son, William.

For the next eighteen years, Franklin's business interests flourished. He published his own newspaper, *The Pennsylvania Gazette*, which remained one of the most influential American newspapers until the end of the century. In 1732 he started printing an **almanac**, which he called *Poor Richard's Almanack*. An almanac and a bible were the most common books in the homes of poorer Americans. Franklin quickly saw this as a chance "for conveying instruction among the common people, who bought scarcely any other books." He filled the spaces between the sections of facts and figures in the almanacs with memorable proverbs discovered through his wide reading, which by now included books in French, Spanish, Italian, German, and Latin—all languages that he had taught himself to read. The familiar saying "Early to bed and early to rise, makes a man healthy, wealthy and wise" was made popular by Franklin, and reflects rather well his style of living during these years.

A portrait of Deborah Read, Franklin's common-law wife, painted around 1758. She was fifteen years old when she first saw the seventeen-year-old Franklin shortly after his arrival in Philadelphia in 1723.

Gaining Knowledge

Franklin, apart from his very brief periods of schooling, was self-taught. He was always very inquisitive, and had a tremendous appetite for knowledge, especially information from books. Even when he was preoccupied with his business, working long hours to make his printing shop the most successful in Philadelphia, he loved to speculate on the forces behind natural phenomena. He observed the behavior of air, clouds, water, and living creatures, and looked for explanations for what he saw. If his friends, or his books, could not provide an answer, then he would work it out himself. One of his great talents as a scientist was his ability to devise simple experiments with homemade apparatus, in order to satisfy his curiosity. There is no doubt that the practical skills he learned in the printing shop were put to good use in these experiments.

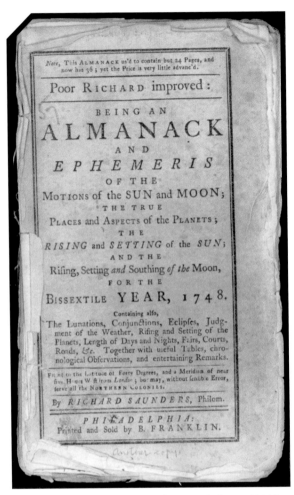

A copy of Poor Richard's Almanack *from 1748. Franklin began publishing the* Almanack *annually in 1733; the final edition was printed in 1758.*

His busy printing and publishing shop left him little time for a social life. If he did have any spare time, Franklin liked to spend it in the company of thoughtful, intelligent people. In 1727 he formed a group that met on a regular basis for a drink or a meal, when they would discuss topics of mutual interest late into the night. Franklin nicknamed this club the Junto—from the Spanish word *junta*, meaning "assembly."

Franklin's growing interest in science and his Junto discussions convinced him that there was a need for all people interested in science to exchange ideas, opinions, and the results of their experiments. In Europe at this time, science was becoming popular, but Franklin saw that its progress was being slowed by the superstitions surrounding natural phenomena, as well as by the vanity of a few scientists who valued their own reputations more than the growth of scientific knowledge.

In 1731 Franklin showed his concern for making knowledge freely available when he founded the first subscription library in Philadelphia. At the time most people in the American colonies had little access to books. There were no public libraries.

So Franklin and about fifty other people, including the members of the Junto club, each invested 40 shillings (the equivalent of about $275 today). The total collected (almost $14,000 in today's dollars) was used to purchase books from London. Subscribers to the library also agreed to pay an additional 10 shillings a year so that additional books could be purchased. The library soon included books on history, geography, science, exploration, poetry, and theology. The subscribers could borrow books from the library freely; non-subscribers could also borrow books if they posted a **surety**, which could be sold if the book wasn't returned. Franklin's library became so popular that by the 1740s similar libraries were formed in other large colonial cities.

The library that Franklin helped to establish in Philadelphia grew so large that it had to move into a bigger space. For many years it rented the second floor of Carpenter's Hall in Philadelphia to hold its collections of books as well as scientific instruments. Today, the Library Company of Philadelphia still exists as a research library.

This portrait of Franklin was painted when his reputation as a businessman and as a leading citizen of Philadelphia was at its height.

To purchase books for the library, Franklin worked with an agent in London named Peter Collinson. They worked together for many years. Collinson was a member of the Royal Society, a scientific organization that had been formed in London in 1660 to encourage discussion of scientific and philosophical affairs. Franklin admired these aims, and in 1743 he published a pamphlet called *A Proposal for Promoting Useful Knowledge*. A year later Franklin and some of his friends from the Junto club formed the American Philosophical Society in Philadelphia. This organization was meant to function in a similar way to London's Royal Society, enabling American scientists to meet and share their discoveries.

Franklin's growing interest in science made him decide to abandon his business career. He looked forward to having "leisure to read, study and make experiments, and converse ... on such points as may produce something for the common benefits of mankind."

A New Direction in Life

In 1748 the *Almanack* sold 10,000 copies—an amazing figure for the time—and Franklin owned not only his Philadelphia printing business, but also shares in printing and publishing shops that he had helped to set up in New York and the West Indies. Then, on this wave of success, aged forty-two, he retired. He was a wealthy man, assured of an income from the business interests that he had left in the hands of his partners. To us it may seem a strange decision for a successful man in the prime of life, who had often preached the virtues of hard work and dedication, to abandon "the little cares and fatigues of business." But for Franklin himself, and for science, it was a fortunate decision.

He could hardly have known that now, halfway through his life, he was poised on the brink of success and worldwide fame in ventures that were very different from those of printing and publishing.

TEXT-DEPENDENT QUESTIONS

1. Where was Benjamin Franklin born?
2. Under what pen name did Franklin write letters published in the *New-England Courant*?
3. What was the name of Franklin's almanac?

 RESEARCH PROJECT

During Benjamin Franklin's lifetime, shortages of money were a problem throughout all of the British colonies in North America. As he gained influence in the Pennsylvania colony, Franklin came up with a solution to the problem. Visit this website maintained by the Federal Reserve Bank of Philadelphia, http://www.philadelphiafed.org/education/teachers/resources/money-in-colonial-times, to find out more about the problems involving coinage and paper money in Colonial America.

This sculpture of Benjamin Franklin operating a printing press is located near City Hall in Philadelphia.

BENJAMIN FRANKLIN - CRAFTSMAN

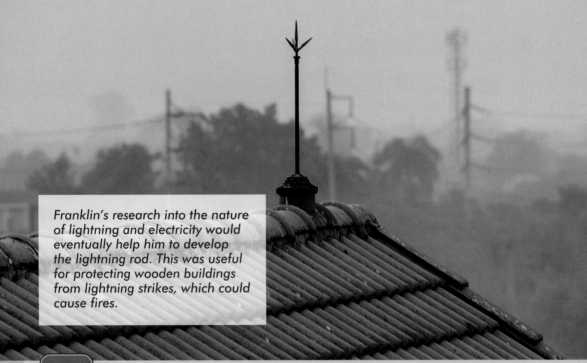

Franklin's research into the nature of lightning and electricity would eventually help him to develop the lightning rod. This was useful for protecting wooden buildings from lightning strikes, which could cause fires.

 WORDS TO UNDERSTAND

amber—a yellow, translucent, fossilized resin, prized by the ancient Greeks.

attraction—a force tending to draw objects together.

capacitor—a device for storing electrical charges.

conductor—a substance that allows electricity to travel from point to point.

electron—one of the three particles which makes up an atom; the nucleus is surrounded by one (in the case of hydrogen) or more electrons that have a negative electric charge.

insulator—a material that does not allow electricity to flow.

Leyden jar—the first device discovered that could store electricity; the forerunner of the capacitor.

magnetite—a type of iron ore that is magnetic.

repulsion—a force tending to drive objects apart.

CHAPTER 2

Franklin and Electricity

Today it is hard to imagine a world without electricity. We depend on it as a source of power to light our homes and businesses, operate machinery, and communicate using cellular phones or computers. But in Franklin's time, electricity was a mere curiosity, a source of entertainment. During the eighteenth century, enterprising electricians could draw crowds to see their tricks. A French electrician entertained King Louis XV and his court by giving an electric shock to 700 monks and making them all jump in the air at once! The age of electrical technology, when electricity could be harnessed to serve mankind through such devices as the electric telegraph, the telephone, and electric light and power, did not begin until the nineteenth century.

Early Electrical Experiments

The first observation of the effects of electricity goes back to ancient times. In those days, **amber** was a highly prized substance among the ancient civilizations of the Mediterranean and the Middle East, because it could be shaped and polished to make attractive ornaments. Amber is a fossilized resin. The Greeks loved ornaments and jewelry made of amber because of its color and luster. They likened it to gold, silver, and other substances that could be burnished, and referred to all these shining, twinkling things as *electron*— "children of the sun." Because of the simple electrical effects shown by amber, the words **electron** and "electricity" found their way into our language.

The ancient Greeks noticed that amber, when rubbed, would attract specks of dust, fur, or small feathers. We can see this same effect by combing our hair

Fig. III.

Fig. IIII.

Tangens 2291816

Fig. VI.

Fig. V.

This illustration is from a book by Otto von Guericke about his electrical experiments that was published in 1672 in Amsterdam. Guericke's electric-generating machine is shown in the lower image.

vigorously with a plastic comb—afterward the comb can pick up small pieces of paper or dust. For a long time this power of **attraction** was confused with magnetism. The ancient Greeks knew that an iron ore called **magnetite** would draw small pieces of iron toward it. This magnetic quality was put to use in the Middle Ages, when pieces of magnetite (then called lodestone) were used to make the first compasses for navigation, after it was realized that a magnet that is free to swing about always comes to rest pointing north and south.

In 1600 William Gilbert, who had been a personal physician to Queen Elizabeth I, published an important book, written in Latin, called *De Magnete* ("Concerning the Magnet"). It was an account of his detailed investigations of magnetism. As it was thought that amber and certain other substances were magnetic, because they attracted particles in the same way as lodestone, these

WILLIAM GILBERT

The English physician and physicist William Gilbert (1544–1603) is sometimes called the "father of electrical engineering." A well-known doctor in London, he was the personal physician to Queen Elizabeth I from 1601 to 1603. He created a magnetized model of the Earth that he called "terrella," in order to experiment on the nature of magnetism. Among other things, he proposed that the core of the Earth was iron, and that this caused the magnetic attraction of a compass needle to the pole. He also studied static electricity, and developed a scientific instrument that could be used to detect the presence of an electric charge, called the "versorium," to help with his experiments. These experiments and his findings were published in his major scientific work, *De Magnete*, in 1600. Gilbert died in 1603, probably of the Plague.

William Gilbert, who published his famous book De Magnete, in 1600. It was the first systematic study of magnetic and electrical effects.

were included in the book. We now know that these substances are not magnetic. Gilbert eventually saw that magnetism was a completely different phenomenon from the behavior of substances like amber, which he called *electrica*. He was the first to point out that pieces of *electrica*, unlike lodestone, had no tendency whatever to align themselves with the earth's north and south poles.

About fifty years after Gilbert's death, another Englishman, Sir Thomas Browne, introduced the term "electricity" to describe the phenomena that he was investigating. By this time, interest in electricity was growing rapidly and distinguished men like Robert Boyle and Isaac Newton experimented with it. Boyle observed that electrical effects worked even in a vacuum, while Newton proved that electrical attraction could take place through plate glass.

In 1660 a German physicist called Otto von Guericke made the first electric-generating machine. It was simply a ball of sulphur fitted to an axle. As it turned, the experimenter placed his hand on it, the resulting friction electrifying the

Scan here to see a modern version of Otto von Guericke's machine:

sulphur, and the experimenter! It quite simply mechanized the process of rubbing the electric substance by hand.

Electrical effects can produce **repulsion** as well as attraction. This was first noticed in 1630 by an Italian investigator. He saw that light objects, initially drawn toward an electrified substance (attraction), would be pushed away immediately after touching it (repulsion). In the seventeenth century, scientists believed electricity to be an invisible fluid produced when electrical materials were rubbed. The discovery of repulsion was explained by the existence of two sorts of fluid. The French philosopher and priest Jean-Antoine Nollet (1700–1770) imagined that an electrified object had two streams of fluid—one flowing away from it, the other flowing into it. Attraction or repulsion of light objects took place when they were caught in one of these streams of fluid.

New Discoveries

The idea that electricity could travel through certain materials, which we now call **conductors**, was not proved until the early part of the eighteenth century. An English scientist named Stephen Gray set up wires that were several hundred feet long and demonstrated electrical effects at opposite ends of the wire. An electrified piece of glass touching one end would make very light pieces of brass foil move about at the other end. Attempts to repeat the experiment using silk thread instead of wire failed. For the first time it became clear that the electric fluid—whatever it was—could travel. Though nobody knew why, certain materials would conduct electricity, allowing it to move through them, whereas other materials would prevent the transmission of electricity. These materials became known as **insulators**.

The most significant advance in electrical science was made in the year that Franklin himself became interested in the subject, 1746. The previous year, a German scientist named Georg von Kleist had discovered that if he held an electrified glass jar, half full of water, in one hand and touched the surface of the water with a metal rod held in his other hand, he received quite a sharp shock. He told some Dutch associates working at the University of Leyden, Andreas Cuneaus and Pieter van Musschenbroek, what he had learned. The two men perfected the device, which became known as a **Leyden jar**, to create a primitive sort of **capacitor** that could hold an electrical charge until it was needed.

Electrical science was now poised for a new leap forward. These improved ways of producing and storing electricity left experimenters with a wider range of possibilities. The fact that large amounts of electricity could be stored meant that large sparks could be made and unfortunate victims could be given shocks. Dramatic public demonstrations became widespread in Europe. There was a new wave of interest in electricity, which soon reached North America and Benjamin Franklin himself.

In 1746 Franklin was on a visit to Boston when he witnessed a public demonstration of electrical effects. This was performed by a Doctor Spence who had recently arrived from Scotland. Though Spence's skill was limited and his equipment crude, Franklin was surprised and delighted at what he saw and soon wrote to tell Peter Collinson in London all about it.

In Europe, electricity had already become a topic of unrivalled scientific interest and a British physician named William Watson had caused quite a stir among British philosophers with some new experiments and theories to explain the results. Collinson responded quickly to Franklin's news and sent him copies of

Three Leyden jars from the eighteenth century. The outsides are covered with thin metal foil, and the conductor at the top of each jar passes down through a cork into the lead shot or water inside the jar.

William Watson (1715–1787) was an English physician and scientist who experimented with electricity during the 1740s. He supported Franklin's discoveries, and the two men had a friendship based on mutual respect. Watson became president of the Royal Society in 1772.

Watson's books, along with a glass tube similar to the one used by Watson in his experiments. Within two years, Franklin was on the verge of discoveries that transformed the contemporary understanding of electricity.

TEXT-DEPENDENT QUESTIONS

1. What was magnetite called in the Middle Ages?
2. What English scientist introduced the term "electricity" around 1650?
3. Who created the Leyden jar?

RESEARCH PROJECT

Choose one of the following scientists who made important discoveries related to electricity before Benjamin Franklin: William Gilbert, Thomas Browne, Robert Boyle, Isaac Newton, Otto von Guericke, Stephen Gray, or Father Jean-Antoine Nollet. Using the internet or your school library, do some research on this scientist. Write a two-page report on his life and accomplishments, and share it with your class.

This portrait of Franklin working in his office as lightning strikes outside the window was painted in 1762.

 ## WORDS TO UNDERSTAND

electrochemical—the interaction of electricity with chemical effects.

electrostatics—the study of the behavior and effects of electric charges.

negative—the electrical state resulting from an excess of electrons; electrons flow away from the negative side of a battery or dynamo.

positive—in electrical terms, the opposite of negative.

CHAPTER 3

Sparks and Lightning

William Watson, who performed electrical experiments in London during the 1740s, described the most important part of his apparatus as "a glass tube, about two foot long, the bore about an inch in diameter." This tube, when rubbed vigorously with a piece of silk, provided the electricity for his experiments. He also emphasized the importance of warming and drying the glass thoroughly beforehand, to prevent the electricity from leaking away.

Franklin received a similar tube from his friend and library agent in London, Peter Collinson. Because Franklin had observed Doctor Spence's demonstration in Boston, he was able to copy the simple Leyden jar that Spence had used to store an electrical charge. Franklin eagerly started his own experiments, with the help of three friends from the American Philosophical Society: Ebenezer Kinnersley, Thomas Hopkinson, and Philip Syng. He soon mastered the sort of tricks performed by Doctor Spence, and before long Franklin's house was one of Philadelphia's major attractions, visited by a steady stream of citizens curious to see the latest wonders of electricity.

New Experiments

Franklin soon tired of repeating experiments merely to entertain the public. He wanted to devise his own experiments and, above all, he wanted to understand the natural forces behind the strange effects. Like all the other natural phenomena that he observed, Franklin wanted to know why things behaved as they did—and electricity was no exception. Early in 1747 he wrote to Collinson announcing that they were making progress. He wrote that he "never before was engaged in any

Franklin owned this static energy generator, which works by rubbing the leather pad against the spinning glass globe to produce a static electrical charge in the globe. This apparatus was used in his experiments and demonstrations.

study that so totally engrossed my attention and my time as this has lately done," and that he had "little leisure for anything else."

By July 1747 Franklin and his three friends were confident that they had made some new discoveries, and wrote in more detail to Collinson. By means of simple, unspectacular experiments, they were able to explain electrical effects in a way that was quite contrary to the general thinking of European scientists of the time. In one experiment, three men stood in row. The first two men stood on sheets of wax, to insulate them from the ground; the third man stood on the ground. The first man, A, held a glass tube, and electrified it by rubbing it with silk; the second man, B, could now draw a small spark from the glass with his finger. The third man, C, could in turn draw a spark from B, showing that electricity had traveled from the glass held by A to B, and then to C. (You might imagine that A, by now, would have no electricity left, but in Franklin's test, C went over to A, and drew a spark from him, which was just as strong as the one he got from B. This showed that even after B took the electricity from A's glass tube, A was still charged.) In the final stage of this experiment, C took no part. A electrified his tube, B touched the tube, and then touched A, when a spark twice as strong as the original was seen.

From this simple experiment, Franklin worked out his explanation of the behavior of electricity. This remains the basis of our modern understanding of **electrostatics**, which is the study of electrically charged bodies, as opposed to electric currents and their effects. Franklin established the Principle of Conservation of Charge, which states that electricity cannot be made; electrical effects are simply due to charges moving from one place to another.

Rather than use the word "charges," Franklin followed his predecessors by referring to a fluid. But where earlier investigators imagined there to be two sorts of fluid, mysteriously produced by rubbing different materials together, Franklin's

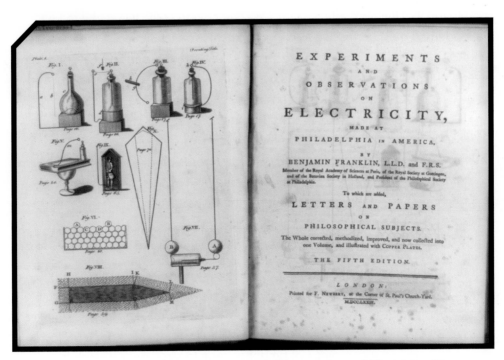

Pages from Franklin's book Experiments and Observations of Electricity. *His discoveries attracted international attention and renown.*

explanation stated that there was just one fluid, a balance of which existed in everything; it could not be created. Electrical effects were, according to Franklin, simply due to a shortage or an excess of the fluid. Franklin was the first to use the words **positive** and **negative** in connection with electricity. In explaining this experiment with the three men A, B, and C, he wrote: "Hence have arisen some new terms among us; we say that B is electricized positively; A negatively. Or rather B is electricized plus and A minus."

Franklin's views were not immediately accepted in Europe. Even six years later Abbé Nollet publicly repudiated them, sticking to his earlier two-fluid idea. But Franklin was undeterred by opposition from traditionalists, and went on to study the Leyden jar in the light of his new theory.

The earliest Leyden jars contained water or lead balls, and it was commonly supposed that they had to be jars simply to contain the elusive electrical fluid. Franklin tried many experiments to find a way of storing more electricity, and soon found that the most effective jar was one covered with thin metal foil on the inside and outside. This led to an experiment in which he found that a glass sheet with lead foil on each side was as effective as a jar, and that by connecting several of these sheets together, he could store even more electricity. He called his array of lead-coated glass sheets the "electrical battery." "Battery" is a term we now use to describe the **electrochemical** power sources used in cell phones, small electronic devices, and motor vehicles. Franklin explained his "battery" by saying that one side was charged positively, the other negatively to the same degree; on discharging it would return to its original state. No charge had been generated—charges had merely been moved about.

Understanding Lightning

Before Franklin's time, other scientists had wondered whether there was any connection between lightning and the puny sparks that they saw in the course of their experiments. In 1716 Isaac Newton wrote to a friend, "I have been much amused by ye singular *phenomena* [Newton's italics] resulting from bringing a needle into contact with a piece of amber or resin fricated on a silke clothe. Ye flame putteth me in mind of sheet lightning on a small—how very small—scale."

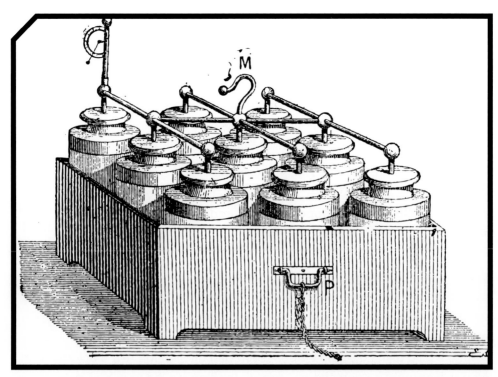

Illustration of Franklin's electric "battery," made up of Leyden jars. Franklin selected the name because the rows of jars reminded him of an artillery battery.

In 1747 Franklin wrote to Collinson that he too was excited by "the wonderful effect of pointed bodies both in drawing off and throwing off the electrical fire." Franklin thought carefully about this, and developed his "doctrine of points." The next time he wrote to Collinson he made this famous suggestion:

> I am of the opinion that houses, ships, and even towers may be effectually secured from the stroke of lightning ... instead of the round balls of wood or metal which are commonly placed on the tops of the weathercocks, vanes or spindles of churches, spires and masts, there should be a rod of iron eight or ten feet in length, sharpened gradually to a point like a needle ... the electrical fire would, I think, be drawn out of a cloud silently before it could come near enough to strike.

Unfortunately, Franklin forgot to say that the rod had to be connected to the ground, and it is just as well that nobody tried out his idea. Franklin soon added the provision of "a wire down the outside of the building into the ground." The lightning conductor, or the Franklin Rod as it was known for many years, had been invented. Even so, it was more than ten years before its use was contemplated in London. Religious people saw the lightning conductor as an interference with nature and God's will. King George III was persuaded that lightning conductors were part of a political plot to destroy the capital's most important buildings. The king chose a team of distinguished scientists, including Franklin, to advise him on this matter. They all assured him that pointed rods were quite safe, so he authorized lightning conductors, but only ones with blunt ends!

But Franklin was still quite a long way from proving that lightning was an electrical phenomenon. In July 1750 he described to Collinson a "sentry box" experiment. He proposed to erect a small hut on top of a high building, with an iron rod leading from the inside of the box to a height of some thirty feet (nine meters) above it. The top end of the rod would, of course, be pointed. Inside the box, he would await a suitable storm cloud and attempt to draw electricity from the rod. He would be perched on an insulated stand in the box, for safety.

To understand Franklin's kite experiment, scan here:

An 1876 illustration shows the popular legend of Franklin's famous "kite" experiment to establish the electrical nature of lightning. The wet string carried electricity down from the kite to a Leyden jar. Franklin was accompanied by his son William, as the illustration shows. However, Franklin did not stand outside in the rain. Instead, he and William stood in a doorway, and Franklin held the kite string with a silk ribbon that they carefully kept dry to avoid electrocution.

DANGEROUS EXPERIMENTS

Franklin and d'Alibard came up with clever experiments to find out more about the nature of electricity. But while they took safety precautions, neither man truly understood how dangerous these experiments could be. Modern scientists have determined that Franklin's kite and damp string probably attracted enough static electricity from the storm to create a spark. But if lightning had actually struck Franklin's kite, he would very likely have been killed.

This happened in 1753 to a German physicist named Georg Wilhelm Richmann who was performing a similar experiment during a thunderstorm in Saint Petersburg, Russia. Richmann was, like Franklin, a respected scientist and a member of the St. Petersburg Academy of Sciences. He wanted to reproduce d'Alibard's experiment, which Franklin had described. However, when Richmann's apparatus, which was similar to d'Alibard's, was struck by lightning, it sent a foot-long spark into Richmann's head that killed him instantly. He may have been the first person in history to die while conducting an electrical experiment.

The Royal Society published the details of Franklin's "sentry box" experiment idea.

Franklin was not the first person to actually try such an experiment. In May of 1752, at Marly, France, a man named Thomas François d'Alibard successfully carried out an experiment similar to the one Franklin had described. He used a tall iron rod to draw static electricity from a storm cloud. A few weeks later, in June 1752, Franklin himself performed the experiment by flying a kite in a

thunderstorm. The kite was not struck directly by lightning—this would have been deadly—but Franklin found that static electricity in the air traveled down the rain-sodden kite string and gave off sparks that could be used to charge a Leyden jar.

Franklin took the precaution of performing his kite experiment well away from the curious gaze of Philadelphia citizens, for fear of the ridicule that would follow failure. He also did not know about d'Alibard's experiment at the time, because of the delay in the time that it took such news to travel between North America and Europe in those days. However, sixteen years later, in 1768, Franklin corresponded with d'Alibard and complimented him on being "the first of Mankind, that had the Courage to attempt drawing Lightning from the Clouds." He referred in passing to "the infinite Pleasure I received in the success of a similar [experiment] I made soon after with a Kite at Philadelphia."

The Modern View

Looking back from the twentieth century, what can we say about Franklin's pioneering work in electrostatics? There is no doubt that his discoveries turned out to be fundamental to our understanding of the nature of electricity—which came about less than 100 years ago.

Toward the end of the nineteenth century, the English physicist J. J. Thomson was investigating the conduction of electricity through tubes containing air at low pressure. (Lightning is simply the passage of electricity through air at normal pressure.) He concluded that electricity was simply the passage of tiny negatively charged particles, which became known as electrons. In 1936, looking back on his own work, and that of Franklin, J. J. Thomson remarked that "A collection of electrons would resemble in many respects Franklin's electric fluid." Later, the discovery of the electron was to be one of the keys that unlocked the understanding of matter itself, through atomic physics. Everything—solids, liquids and gases—consists of atoms. These in turn consist of a positively charged core, made up of protons and neutrons, surrounded by negatively charged electrons, the number of electrons being such that their total negative charge equals the positive charge of the core, known as the nucleus.

The simple electrical phenomena first noticed with amber, and pursued so vigorously by Franklin, can now be explained quite simply by the movement of electrons. Friction between two different materials leaves one with too few, and the other with too many electrons. Too few give a positive charge, and too many give a negative charge. But the electron is fundamental, and cannot be produced, just like Franklin's concept of electricity.

TEXT-DEPENDENT QUESTIONS

1. What three friends helped Franklin with his electrical experiments in the 1740s?
2. What did Franklin find was the most effective Leyden jar?
3. Who was the first person to try Franklin's "sentry box" experiment idea?

RESEARCH PROJECT

Perform this simple experiment to demonstrate the effect of static electricity. You will need a plastic spoon, a tablespoon each of salt and pepper on a paper plate, and a piece of wool. Rub the spoon on the wool vigorously for a minute, then pass it slowly across the paper plate, about an inch above the salt and pepper mixture, and see what happens.

The pepper should adhere to the spoon. This occurs because rubbing the wool with the spoon transfers negative electrons to the spoon. The salt and pepper are positively charged, so they are attracted to the negative charge in the spoon. However, the charge is only strong enough to pull the lighter pepper grains across the distance to the spoon.

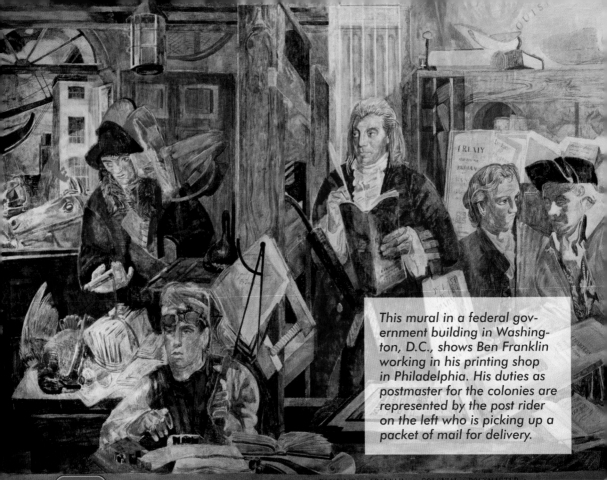

This mural in a federal government building in Washington, D.C., shows Ben Franklin working in his printing shop in Philadelphia. His duties as postmaster for the colonies are represented by the post rider on the left who is picking up a packet of mail for delivery.

 WORDS TO UNDERSTAND

drag—the slowing-down force on an object moving through a fluid, such as a ship through water.

electroconvulsive therapy—the controversial treatment of mental illness by giving patients electric shocks.

fluxion—an old-fashioned mathematical term meaning "a small change"; Franklin's use of it refers to Calculus, a form of mathematics developed by Isaac Newton in the seventeenth century.

hydrodynamics—as aerodynamics, but concerned with the movement of water.

patent—an exclusive legal right to make, sell or exploit a new invention or process.

CHAPTER 4

Schemes, Gadgets, and Observations

The success and lasting significance of Franklin's electrical experiments tend to overshadow some of his other investigations. But, throughout his life, whenever he had a spare moment, his mind would turn to some new problem. Some of his suggestions were quite light-hearted, but at least these give us an insight into the humorous nature of this warm-hearted man.

Even some of his electrical experiments were viewed with a sense of fun. In 1749 he wrote to Peter Collinson suggesting that perhaps one day an "electric banquet" could be held. The turkey for the feast would be killed by an electric shock, and roasted over a fire lit from "electrified bottles" (presumably, he meant something similar to Leyden jars). Perhaps this suggestion was not so light-hearted as it would seem, for, somewhat ironically, the next year he reported that while he was preparing to give an electric shock to a turkey, something went wrong, and he himself got the shock! He was struck to the ground and experienced "a violent shaking of my whole body."

In a more serious context, Franklin became interested in the treatment of certain illnesses by applying electric shocks to the patient. He experimented with discharging Leyden jars against the limbs of people who had lost their use, but found that any benefits did not last long. Franklin was not convinced that any permanent cure could result from this procedure. Today, however, electrical shocks are used to stimulate muscles for people who are rehabilitating from injury. There is another a procedure used for treating people with certain types of mental illnesses, known as **electroconvulsive therapy**. However, modern medical experts disagree over the value of this sort of treatment.

Improving Philadelphia

When Franklin became an established businessman and a respected citizen of Philadelphia, he turned his mind to improving the general living conditions in the town. Philadelphia was one of the largest cities in the American colonies, and like other large cities of the eighteenth century, it was not attractive. All the houses were heated by open log fires, which produced foul pollution of the air. Houses were built of wood, so that the risk of fire was high. The streets were dirty, unpaved, and badly lit, and at night robbers and vagabonds lurked in dark passageways and doorways.

During the 1730s Franklin mounted a campaign for firefighters and equipment through his Pennsylvania Gazette newspaper. In December 1736 he and several friends established a volunteer firefighting brigade, the Union Fire Company, in Philadelphia. It was the first formally organized fire department in the colonies. The Union Fire Company remained active until the 1840s.

SIDEBAR: DAYLIGHT SAVING TIME

Americans today are familiar with the concept of "daylight saving time." We adjust clocks backward or forward by an hour in order to make the best possible use of the amount of daylight available at all times of the year. Benjamin Franklin was the first person to think of such a scheme as a way of saving fuel, in 1784, when he was living in Paris. He was most concerned that Parisians "should have lived so long by the smoky, unwholesome, and enormously expensive light of candles." He suggested that an alteration to the setting of their clocks would enable them to enjoy "pure light of the sun for nothing." However, daylight saving time plans were not implemented in the United States or European countries until the early twentieth century.

Through his printed publications, Franklin campaigned vigorously to change this. He introduced a cheap, effective street lamp that would not become dimmed by soot easily. He pressed for the streets to be paved, and for men to be employed to clean the streets by day and to patrol them at night. To combat the risk of fire, he established America's first fire brigade.

But even with improvements on the way, nighttime Philadelphia was not pleasant, and most citizens preferred to stay at home by the cheerful glow of the open fire. Franklin observed that a lot of the heat and sparks went straight up the chimney; or failing that, a great deal of smoke came back into the room! So, he set to work on a design for an improved fireplace.

In describing his design, Franklin wrote, "so much of the comfort and conveniency of our lives, for so great a part of the year, depends on the article of fire; since Fuel is become so expensive, and (as the country is more clear'd and settled) will of course grow scarcer and dearer, any new proposal for saving the wood ... may at least be worth consideration." His design improved the air supply to the fire, and made sure that the smoke gave up all its heat before going up the chimney. Not only was less fuel used, but sparks were less likely to fly out of the chimney.

Pennsylvania's deputy governor offered to issue a **patent** to Franklin, to prevent other people from copying the new fireplace, called a Franklin stove. This would have allowed Franklin to profit by being the only one who could sell his invention. However, Franklin refused this legal protection because he believed that everyone should benefit from new inventions. He wrote, "as we enjoy great advantages from the inventions of others, we should be glad of an opportunity to serve others by any invention of ours, and this we should do freely and generously." As a result, others were able to use Franklin's design and make it even better.

Making Music

When Franklin was in England for the second time, between 1757 and 1762, he mingled in fashionable London circles, where music was a major part of day-to-day entertainment. In 1762 he wrote to a friend, Giambatista Beccaria, in Italy. Ten years earlier, Beccaria had defended Franklin's ideas on electricity when they were under attack from the scientific establishment. In his letter, Franklin described how he had watched an Irishman named Puckeridge playing tunes on wineglasses by rubbing their rims with his fingers. Each glass had a different level of water, which changed the pitch of the note. However, Franklin wrote, Puckeridge and his glasses were both lost when a fire consumed the house where he was staying. After this, a man named Edmund Delaval tried to recreate the performance with the water-filled glasses before the Royal Society.

Franklin had enjoyed the general effect of the musical glasses so much that he immediately set to work designing an improved version. He mounted the glasses on a long spindle, driven by a treadle, like a sewing machine, and tuned them by grinding away their rims very carefully, comparing the pitch of each one with a "well-tuned harpsichord." The player sat beside the instrument, sounding

Example of a metal Franklin stove fitted into a fireplace in a colonial-era home. A hollow baffle at the back of the stove helped to transfer more heat from the fire into the room, rather than losing the heat up the chimney.

To hear a song played on Franklin's armonica, scan here:

the glasses of his choice by touching them with his water-moistened fingers. Franklin called his invention the *armonica*, and concluded that, "its tones are incomparably sweet beyond those of any other."

For a time, the *armonica* was very popular instrument in Europe. Many famous composers wrote music for the *armonica*, including Wolfgang Amadeus Mozart and Ludwig Beethoven. However, by the 1830s the *armonica* mostly disappeared from use, in part because it was hard to play and the glasses were too fragile.

Endless Observations

Franklin's observations of natural phenomena and his subsequent deductions and conjectures were endless. While it is true to say that he did not give any one topic the same detailed attention as he gave to electricity, his written accounts of his investigations establish his reputation as a scientific thinker of the highest caliber.

During his last visit to England, Franklin spent a short time over in Holland. He traveled about the flat countryside by canal, in the typical flat-bottomed Dutch barges drawn by horses. One day, he noticed that his barge was traveling more slowly than usual, and wondered why; the boatman told him that it had been a

Franklin once wrote that of all his inventions, "the glass armonica has given me the greatest personal satisfaction." A foot-pedal turned the spindle on which the glass bowls were placed, and the performer pressed his water-dampened fingers onto the spinning bowl to create the instrument's haunting sound.

dry summer, and the water was low. Was the barge dragging along the bottom of the canal? The boatman said that it was not.

Back in London, Franklin questioned some Thames bargemen, and they all agreed that their boats were slower when the river was low. So Franklin devised an experiment to unravel the mystery. He built a model canal, fourteen feet (four meters) long and six inches (fifteen centimeters) wide, and a model barge to be pulled along the canal by a cord leading over a pulley to a weight. He timed his barge as it was drawn along, and found that when he did not have much water in his model canal, the barge went more slowly, even though the weight pulling it along was unchanged. This experiment marked the beginning of **hydrodynamics**, the study of water flow around obstructions. In modern terms, we would explain Franklin's observation by saying that the flow of water beneath the barge was impeded by the closeness of the bottom of the canal, causing **drag**.

Franklin also observed the calming effect of "oil on troubled waters" and actually carried out quite large-scale experiments, with friends from the Royal Society, on the pond at Clapham Common in South London, and on the Solent off Portsmouth. He even learned that fishermen could find herring shoals by looking for patches of sea made smooth by oil released from the herrings' skins.

Air movements, mists, and clouds interested Franklin greatly, and he was particularly fascinated by whirlwinds and waterspouts. In 1753 he wrote to a friend putting forward a rather complicated explanation for these phenomena. As it turned out, he was incorrect on this occasion, but his letter shows that he was quite aware that he could be wrong, as he ended with the words: "If my hypothesis is not the truth itself it is least as naked: For I have not with some of our learned moderns, disguis'd my nonsense in Greek, cloth'd it in algebra or adorn'd it with **fluxions**."

TEXT-DEPENDENT QUESTIONS

1. Why did Franklin decline the offer to patent his stove invention?
2. What musical instrument did Franklin invent in the 1760s?
3. What did Franklin built a model canal to study?

RESEARCH PROJECT

Using your school library or the internet, do some research on what life was like in colonial Philadelphia during the 1730s and 1740s. What improvements did Benjamin Franklin suggest, and how did they improve the living conditions in the city? Write a two-page report and share it with your class.

Schooners like this one sailed between North America and England in Franklin's time. On several of his Atlantic voyages, Franklin engaged his curiosity by studying the ocean.

WORDS TO UNDERSTAND

bioluminescence—the dim light given off by creatures that live far beneath the sea, where it is perpetually dark.

oceanography—the scientific study of the seas.

plankton—small or microscopic organisms that drift or float in the sea, including protozoans, small crustaceans, and the eggs and larval stages of larger marine animals. Whales and other sea creatures are adapted to feed on plankton, especially by filtering the water.

CHAPTER 5

Pioneering Oceanographer

Between 1753 and 1774, Franklin was deputy postmaster general of North America, even though he lived in England from 1764 to 1775. In 1769 the British postal authorities asked him to find out why American mail ships always crossed the Atlantic more quickly than the British ones. Franklin observed that, "A vessel from Europe to North America may shorten her passage by avoiding to stem the stream, in which the thermometer will be very useful; and a vessel from America to Europe may do the same by the same means of keeping in it. It may have happened accidentally that voyages have been shortened by these circumstances. It is well to have command of them."

The reasons behind this investigation were political. Clashes between the new American colonies and the more traditional government in England were reaching their peak. No time could be lost in getting messages across the Atlantic. The crossing took about six weeks—and political advantage could be won or lost if the mail was delayed by only a day or two.

"The stream" that Franklin refers to is the Gulf Stream. This is a current of warm water that flows from the Gulf of Mexico along the Atlantic coast of North America. It crosses the Atlantic and eventually reaches the shores of Western Europe. Modern methods of measuring temperatures and currents have allowed scientists to plot the course of the Gulf Stream accurately, and to understand its causes and how it affects our climate. But Franklin deserves credit for having

Whalers from Nantucket Island, including Franklin's cousin Timothy Folger, had experience with Atlantic currents, as they had to account for them when traveling to and from the whaling grounds in the Arctic Ocean.

first investigated "the stream." He was the first man to carry out systematic measurements of the temperature of the water and to publish a chart of its path and location.

Starting an Investigation

In his investigations of the Gulf Stream, Franklin first sought the advice of Captain Timothy Folger, who lived on Nantucket and was related to Franklin's mother, Abiah. For years Folger had commanded whaling ships off the eastern coast of North America. His reply to Franklin's enquiry from England confirmed that there was something distinctly unusual about the behavior of the sea along the Atlantic coastline.

Folger was certainly aware of the tactics used by the American mail ship skippers, in trying to shorten the time taken for their crossings. As a whale hunter, he knew that whales were only found in certain areas, but he didn't really understand why. Captain Folger described to Franklin a zone where there were no whales. It turned out that this was the area of warmer sea water within the Gulf Stream. Whales feed on microscopic creatures called **plankton**, which are found in largest numbers in cold seas. There is much less plankton in the warm

In 1781, Benjamin Franklin attended a concert in which he narrowly escaped death when the opera house caught fire and burned.

For amazing facts about Benjamin Franklin, scan here:

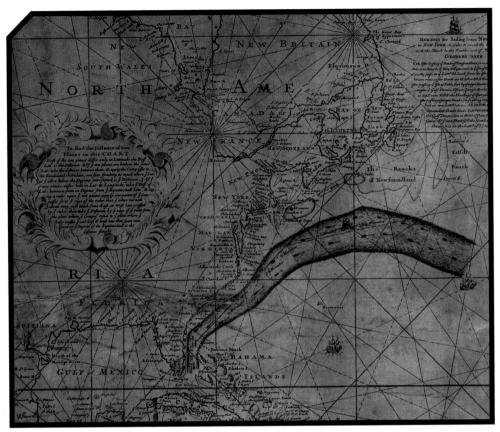

Detail of the chart Franklin and Timothy Folger prepared in 1769 showing the Gulf Stream, which begins near Florida and flows north along the Atlantic coast.

Gulf Stream, which explains why Captain Folger saw no whales there.

When Folger replied to Franklin, he enclosed a chart marking these areas. He also sketched the routes taken by American mail-ship captains that had allowed the quickest crossing of the Atlantic. A vessel sailing to England would sail straight up the east coast of North America and follow the Gulf Stream across to England. But on the return journey, she would steer a zig-zag path when nearing the east coast. Franklin realized that this was the best way to deal with the current. On the eastbound trip, it obviously helped the captain to stay in the Gulf Stream and take advantage of the strong current. But when sailing west, a captain would have to cut smartly across it so that the current would not slow his ship down.

On October 29, 1769, Franklin sent his findings to the postal authorities. Unfortunately, at least for the British, his advice fell upon deaf ears. In Franklin's own words, the British sea captains "slighted it." There the matter rested for six years. Franklin was not discouraged by the British captains' failure to heed his advice. His ever-lively scientific curiosity was aroused, though frustrated. It was not until 1775 that he was to go back across the Atlantic, giving him the opportunity to have a closer look at the Gulf Stream.

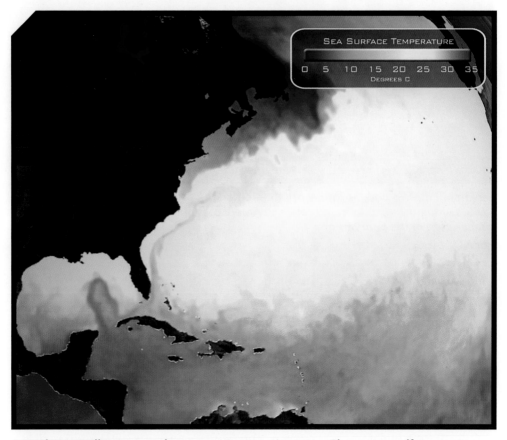

A modern satellite image showing water temperatures. The warm gulf stream is clearly visible along the coast of the southern United States, before coming into contact with colder Arctic waters and dispersing into the Atlantic.

Benjamin Franklin and his family are greeted on their return to Philadelphia in 1785. During the voyage from France to America, Franklin diligently studied the temperature of the Gulf Stream.

A Closer Look

Early in 1775 Franklin was coming to the end of a ten-year turn of duty representing the American colonies to the British government. He had been deeply involved in the political difficulties between the colonies and Britain that began in the mid-1760s. To Franklin, it looked as if a peaceful way out of the difficulties was impossible. Downhearted at the prospect of bloodshed in the colonies, he felt that there was no point in being away from America any longer.

On March 21, 1775, Franklin set sail from Portsmouth, bound for Pennsylvania.

His grandson, Temple, was with him. The crossing was to take six weeks in, as he later wrote, "weather so moderate." Most of his time on the voyage was spent in writing an account of his time in England. But as they approached North America, his thoughts turned again to the Gulf Stream. So, from the third week in April, almost up to the end of the voyage on the 5th of May, he busied himself by carefully studying the nature of the sea in the areas shown on Captain Folger's chart. He reported that the water in those areas appeared to be a different color and, unlike the rest of the North Atlantic, did not sparkle at night. These observations match our present-day knowledge of plankton. The apparent color of seawater depends on how clear it is, and the clarity is affected by the amount of plankton in it. The sparkling Franklin referred to is phosphorescence or **bioluminescence**—a natural light given off by some sea creatures at night when they come to the surface to feed.

Most importantly, Franklin constantly measured the temperature of the sea as they sailed west. From seven in the morning, until eleven at night, he lowered his thermometer into the sea many times a day. He established that the Gulf Stream was several degrees warmer than the surrounding ocean. Strangely enough, perhaps as if to remind Franklin of his correspondence with his whale-hunting cousin, he sighted a whale on the edge of the warm-water zone, but it was the only one seen during the entire voyage.

EXPLORING THE GULF STREAM

In 1969, two hundred years after Franklin's investigation, a team of six oceanographers drifted for six weeks in a small submarine beneath the surface of the Gulf Stream. Their aim was to add to our knowledge of the Gulf Stream, and in honor of their predecessor, they named the research submarine *Ben Franklin*.

On May 16, 1775, Franklin wrote to the English chemist Joseph Priestley, modestly saying that he had made "a valuable philosophical discovery which I shall communicate to you when I get a little time." He did not get "a little time" until ten years later, when his public life was nearly at an end and he was on another journey from Europe to America.

In August and September 1785, aged nearly eighty, Franklin was returning from France, where he had represented the colonies during and after the American Revolution. He again kept daily records of air and water temperatures as his ship crossed the Atlantic. On two occasions Franklin tried to measure the temperature nine or ten meters under the surface, by lowering a container to that depth and swiftly hoisting it back aboard. Franklin's investigations set the scene for the development of the important science of **oceanography** in the next two centuries.

TEXT-DEPENDENT QUESTIONS

1. Why did the British government want to know why American mail ships crossed the Atlantic more quickly than British ones?

2. What Nantucket sea captain gave Franklin important information about currents in the Atlantic Ocean?

3. What did Franklin do constantly as his ship sailed west across the Atlantic in April and May of 1775?

RESEARCH PROJECT

The Gulf Stream has an important role to play in regulating the world's climate. To find out more about it, read the article from Columbia University's Earth Institute at: http://blogs.ei.columbia.edu/2017/06/06/could-climate-change-shut-down-the-gulf-stream.

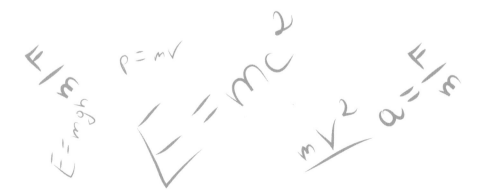

This portrait of Benjamin Franklin was painted in 1767, while he was representing the American colonies in London.

 WORDS TO UNDERSTAND

Crown colony—a form of British colonial administration in which the colony is ruled by a governor appointed by the king.

mesmerized—hypnotized, or in a trance; the word is derived from the name of the Austrian doctor Anton Mesmer, whose false claims for his hypnotic methods were investigated by Franklin.

Quakers—the common name for the Society of Friends, a religious group formed in the seventeenth century.

CHAPTER 6

An American in Europe

When Franklin retired from business in 1748, he dreamt of happy, peaceful years ahead. He imagined that he would have all the time in the world to pursue his favorite interests, to read and write about them, to discuss them with his friends and to devise experiments. But this was not to be. Because he had a strong sense of responsibility toward his fellow citizens and a unique ability to solve problems, he became drawn into the turbulent politics that accompanied America's emergence as a new nation.

The Changing Colonies

When Franklin was young, the British controlled thirteen colonies in North America. They were populated by immigrants from Europe who had fled from religious or political oppression or, like Franklin's own father, from poverty. Many of these immigrants had a fierce ambition to make a success of their new lives in America. As the population of the colonies grew, so did their importance to the British Empire as a source of natural resources.

In 1747, the year in which he first became interested in electricity, Franklin had a foretaste of the problems to come. At the time Great Britain was at war with France and Spain, both of which also controlled colonies in North America. In fact, both Britain and France claimed some of the same lands, so there were often opportunities for fighting. The colonists in Pennsylvania were concerned that the French or their Native American allies would attack frontier towns in the colony. Franklin worked to create a volunteer defense association to guard against the threat. There was little help from the British government, and Franklin also encountered great opposition from the **Quakers**, a pacifist religious group that was prominent in the Pennsylvania colony.

The war ended with a treaty signed in Europe and the threat of invasion passed. Franklin returned to his study of electricity, and during this period he made some of his most remarkable discoveries. But within a few years, war again threatened the colonies. Tensions between Britain and France were rising, and soon would flare up into a worldwide conflict known as the Seven Years' War. In North America, the conflict was known as the French and Indian War.

In 1754, representatives of six colonies met in Albany, New York, to discuss working together to defend against Native American raids in the west, as well

This illustration published in Franklin's Pennsylvania Gazette *in May 1754 was a warning to the British colonies in America that they would have to work together against the French and Native Americans.*

By virtue of a royal charter granted by King Charles II (seated) in 1681, William Penn (standing, right) and his descendants became the proprietors of the Pennsylvania colony, with the right to sell or rent land and receive taxes on their property. The Penns in turn paid the royal treasury a share of their earnings, but otherwise had free reign to operate the colony. The Penn family lived in England and rarely visited the colony, which led to disagreements between the Penns and the elected legislature.

as against the increasing threat of piracy along the Atlantic coast. Franklin urged the colonies to band together in self-defense, but his pleas fell on deaf ears. He proposed that local taxes could pay for an adequate defense force, which would make the colonies less dependent on London for their own defense. But the colonies were too proud and suspicious of their neighbors to give up any of their independence. Franklin was ignored.

During the French and Indian War, Franklin was elected to command a militia company that was formed to defend settlements in western Pennsylvania. In January 1756, he led his troops to a small frontier settlement called Gnadenhütten, in Pennsylvania's Lehigh Valley, where Native Americans allied with the French had attacked and killed more than a dozen people. Franklin's men warded off enemy attacks on the way to the settlement. He oversaw construction of several small wooden stockades, similar to the one pictured, to defend the area from subsequent attacks. Franklin also led patrols against enemy forces, before returning to Philadelphia in March.

Representative in England

In 1757, the Pennsylvania Assembly sent Franklin to London to represent its interests before the British government. At the time, the Penn family controlled the entire colony of Pennsylvania. In 1681 William Penn had received a royal charter giving him control over Pennsylvania from the king; after his death, his sons took over management of the colony. There was a colonial Assembly, whose members were elected to represent the people, but it had little power. Thomas and Richard Penn cared little for the colony or its inhabitants; they were most interested in receiving a good income from their property.

To raise money to defend the colony, the Assembly wanted to tax the Penn brothers' lands. However, the Penns would have to agree to this. The Assembly chose Franklin to go to London to discuss matters with the Penn brothers. His dealings with them were unfruitful, for they were suspicious of the Assembly and of Franklin himself. They saw him as a troublemaker, especially as he was popular enough to have formed a local militia.

Franklin stayed on in London, enjoying his contacts with well-known figures from science, the arts, and politics. With Britain and France at war, it was not safe to cross the Atlantic. He was not able to return to America until 1762.

Two years later, he was back in London, once again to discuss disagreements involving the Penn family and the Pennsylvania Assembly. The Assembly wanted Franklin to press the British government to take the Penns' colony away from them and to turn it into a **Crown colony**. Again, his proposals were ignored.

In the meantime, the end of the French and Indian War, as well as the larger Seven Years' War, brought about many changes. The British had gained control of New France, and it became the fourteenth British colony: Canada. To preserve peace with the Native Americans, in 1763 the British king decreed that immigrants could not settle lands to the west. And the British Parliament determined that the colonies should pay toward their own defense, and began to impose new taxes on the American colonies.

One of the first of these was the Stamp Act of 1765. This imposed an extra charge on every legal document issued in America. However, many Americans

The Stamp Act of 1765 required tax stamps to be purchased and attached to all legal documents, permits, contracts, newspapers, pamphlets, and playing cards in the American colonies. The money raised from this tax was to be used to help pay the cost of protecting the colonies.

were upset about the tax. Unlike taxpayers in England, who were represented in Parliament, the Americans had very little say in how the money was spent. Franklin expressed the American view of the tax so forcefully that the Stamp Act was repealed the next year. Though this made Franklin a national hero in America, he was still distressed by the fact that no representatives from the colonies were allowed to take seats in Parliament, and he saw far worse disagreements ahead.

Franklin stayed in London for another nine years, trying to calm disagreements between the colonies and the British government. He was in a difficult position. Some Americans who wanted total independence were talking of revolution and bloodshed. Franklin was striving for a peaceful settlement, with a ban on trade with England as the most severe weapon to be used by the colonies. This moderate point of view did not go down well with the revolutionaries. At the same time, Franklin was becoming unpopular with the government in London. King George III and his ministers were unhappy with Franklin and his constant defense of the colonies.

Benjamin Franklin stands before the British Privy Council on January 29, 1774. As a representative of Pennsylvania's legislature, Franklin had tried to peacefully resolve the growing disagreements between British and colonial leaders. However, at this government hearing, Franklin was unfairly accused of instigating the Boston Tea Party and other rebellious activities. This incident helped Franklin realize that the Americans would never have the same rights as other British citizens.

Franklin was returning to America when clashes between American militiamen and British troops occurred at Lexington and Concord, Massachusetts, on April 19, 1775.

The year 1773 saw the notorious Boston Tea Party incident, when sixteen citizens, dressed up as Mohawk Indians, threw chests of valuable tea, bound for England, into the harbor in Boston. The Boston Tea Party was a protest by the Americans against a tax on tea—even though the tax was very small, Americans refused to pay. The next year, as a punishment, Boston Harbor was closed by an Act of Parliament. Franklin, always seeking a reasonable settlement, deplored both the tea-dumping and the harsh reprisal.

War for Independence

By 1775 Franklin realized that the differences between London and the colonies could not be settled, and he decided to return home. While he was sailing across the Atlantic, American and British troops fired on each other at Lexington and Concord. The clash that Franklin had dreaded for so long had happened.

Though he was now sixty-nine years old, Franklin did not abandon the American cause. He realized that revolution was necessary. He was among the delegates sent by the colonies to the Second Congressional Congress in Philadelphia during the spring and summer of 1776. Along with Thomas Jefferson and several others, Franklin helped to write the Declaration of Independence, which was adopted on July 4 and publicly read on July 8.

At the end of 1776, Franklin was in Paris. The war with England was now in earnest, and Franklin had secretly been sent to ask the French to help the colonies gain their independence. At first King Louis XVI was reluctant. Though he wished to thwart Britain's empire, he disliked the idea of helping subjects oppose a

Members of the committee assigned to draft the Declaration of Independence—John Adams, Roger Sherman, Robert Livingston, Thomas Jefferson, and Benjamin Franklin—present the document to John Hancock, president of the Second Continental Congress, in June 1776.

THOMAS JEFFERSON

Thomas Jefferson was thirty-three years old when he joined Benjamin Franklin and three other members of the Second Continental Congress as part of the Committee of Five, which was assigned the task of writing the Declaration of Independence. Jefferson was a lawyer, scholar, and owner of a 5,000-acre plantation in Virginia.

Franklin and Jefferson had many things in common. Both shared a deep interest in science, and a desire to understand the world around them. Both were prolific writers. Like Franklin, Jefferson was an inventor as well as a supporter of education. They soon formed a friendship that would last until Franklin's death in 1790.

During the War for Independence, Jefferson served a term as governor of Virginia. After the war, Jefferson had an opportunity to work with Franklin again when he was assigned to take over as the diplomat who represented the United States to the French government. Franklin had been working in France for more than seven years by the time Jefferson arrived in August 1874. The two men worked together for nine months before Franklin returned to America. Jefferson would later write that during the transition, he was

fellow monarch. But Franklin was incredibly popular in France, and he used his charm and political skill to persuade French leaders to support the Americans. After the American army defeated the British at Saratoga in late 1778, the French agreed to supply the colonists with weapons and money. France's allies, Spain and Holland, also agreed to support the Americans.

With French assistance, the war turned in the Americans' favor. In October 1781, asked, "Is it you, sir, who replaces Doctor Franklin?" Jefferson replied, "No one can replace him, sir; I am only his successor."

Jefferson would return to the United States in 1789, when President George Washington appointed him secretary of state. He was elected to a term as vice president to John Adams in 1796, then was elected president in 1800. Under President Jefferson, the nation expanded its borders through the Louisiana Purchase. Thirteen future states would be

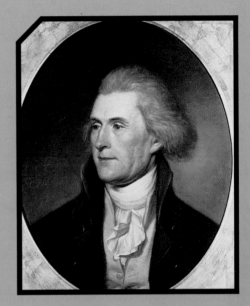

formed out of the western territory that Jefferson obtained from France for about $15 million. Jefferson died on July 4, 1826—the fiftieth anniversary of the signing of the Declaration of Independence.

a major British army in the South, commanded by General Charles Cornwallis, surrendered to George Washington's troops at Yorktown. This marked the final major battle of the war. But for Franklin, the peace negotiations dragged on for two more years. When the formal treaty was signed in September 1783, he wrote: "May we never see another war! For in my opinion there never was a good war or a bad peace."

To learn about Franklin's diplomatic work in Paris, scan here:

By the time the Treaty of Paris was signed in September 1783, Franklin's health was beginning to fail. He was seventy-seven years old, but he refused to be idle. His powers of observation and analysis, and his wit, were as sharp as ever.

As America's chief representative in Europe, Franklin had a few duties left to carry out, mostly in negotiating trade agreements. But he had much more spare time, especially after an American consul was sent to Paris. Franklin lived in a small hotel in Passy, near the fashionable Bois de Boulogne. As in London years before, his friends were prominent philosophers, scientists, writers and politicians. He revived his old printing skills, and set up a small press, on which he would print his "bagatelles," which were short humorous pieces, generally written to delight his lady friends. Franklin even published a pamphlet entitled "Information for Those who would Remove to America," intended for would-be immigrants to the new country. Franklin pointed out that the New World was not for the faint-hearted; immigrants would only be made welcome if they were prepared to work hard. America, he wrote, was not a land where "the fowls fly around ready roasted, crying 'come and eat me!'"

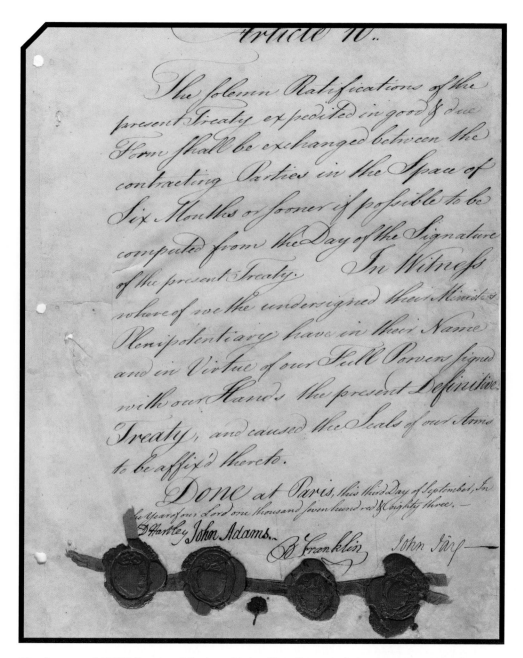

Final page of 1783 Treaty of Paris, which officially ended the American War for Independence. The treaty was signed by American diplomats John Adams, Benjamin Franklin, and John Jay, as well as British government representative David Hartley.

Final Years

At the end of 1783 Franklin was excited by the first balloon flights, which took place near his home. He actually witnessed the first manned ascent, when the Montgolfier brothers went aloft in their hot air balloon. He recalled that a Frenchman beside him in the crowd said to him, "But what good is it?" Franklin replied, "Of what good is a newborn baby?" He even speculated about the role that aircraft could take in warfare, and later wrote "Convincing sovereigns of the folly of wars may perhaps be one effect of it; since it will be impracticable for the most potent of them to guard his domain."

In 1784 Franklin was invited to join a team of distinguished French scientists who were investigating the activities of an Austrian physician named Anton Mesmer. Mesmer had devised a form of medical treatment that relied upon "animal magnetism." His methods had been discredited in Vienna and Berlin, but in Paris, the enthusiasm among the gentry and nobility was verging on hysteria. Franklin and his team exposed Mesmer as a greedy and unscrupulous impostor, and concluded that his

An engraving of Franklin made when he was in Paris between 1776 and 1785. Unlike the fashionable Parisians of the time, who wore powdered wigs, Franklin simply wore a fur cap to protect his bald head from the cold.

Franklin is seated at the center of this painting of the Constitutional Convention, which was held in Philadelphia in 1787. Standing at the left is George Washington, who had been asked to preside over the convention. Its task was to create a new framework of government for the United States. Franklin's major accomplishments were to help soothe disagreements between the delegates.

claims of being able to cure most known ailments were false. Even so, the word **mesmerized**, meaning "hypnotized," or "in a trance," is in our language to this day.

Franklin's ingenuity did not leave him in his last years. To help himself overcome the infirmities of his old age, he invented bifocal spectacles, a mechanical hand to reach for books on the top shelves of his library, and a fan, worked by his feet, to keep cool while reading.

He traveled home to Philadelphia for the last time in 1785, arriving there on September 14. He was pleased to be home, but he was not to be left in peace for long. His political wisdom and good sense were still in demand. In 1787 he was called to a convention in Philadelphia to draw up a constitution for the future government of the United States of America. The system of government that had been created during the War for Independence, known as the Articles of Confederation, was awkward and many Americans felt a new framework of government was needed. However, delegates to the convention had many ideas and disagreements. Franklin pleaded with all factions to be reasonable, and in a speech told them, "When a broad table is to be made, and the edges of the planks do not fit, the artist takes a little from both and makes a good join. In like manner here both sides must part with some of their demands." Ultimately the convention produced the Constitution of the United States, which with some modifications has been the framework of government for more than 230 years.

Franklin's work at the Constitutional Convention marked his last major public appearance. During the last two years of his life, he was troubled with a painful illness. Near the end, he had to be given opium to relieve his distress. But he complained little, and said that he was grateful to have lived long enough to see this turbulent spell of American history come to a satisfactory conclusion.

Benjamin Franklin died on April, 17, 1790, leaving his mark on a wide range of human activities. To this day the influence of his work, and thought, remains in science and technology, publishing, education, national and international politics, medicine and public health, and humanities. But above all he was a modern man, and his way of thinking, his adaptability, and his energy helped to shape the world we live in today.

TEXT-DEPENDENT QUESTIONS

1. What did Franklin propose to colonial leaders in 1754?
2. Why did the Pennsylvania Assembly send Franklin to London in 1757?
3. Where was Franklin sent at the end of 1776? Why was he sent there?

RESEARCH PROJECT

Benjamin Franklin and the other delegates who signed the Declaration of Independence pledged to each other "our Lives, our Fortunes, and our sacred Honor." Create a list of all the men who signed the declaration, and look up each one in an encyclopedia to find out what sort of price they paid for their commitment to the Patriot cause. Were any of them killed or captured by British soldiers? How many lost family members to the war? Did any of them benefit in a material way from independence, and if so, how?

Chronology

1706
Benjamin Franklin born in Boston, Massachusetts, on January 17.

1714
Attends grammar school.

1715
Taught by Mr. Brownell

1716
Assists his father in the soap and candle making trade.

1718
Apprenticed to his brother in his printing business.

1721
James Franklin's newspaper, the *New-England Courant,* founded.

1722
Benjamin Franklin writes his "Silence Dogood" articles.

1723
Flees to Philadelphia and works as a printer.

1725
Arrives in London.

1726
Returns to Philadelphia.

1727
First meetings of the Junto.

1730
Runs his own printing shop; Deborah Read becomes his wife.

1731
First son, William, born; the subscription "Library Company" formed.

1732
Second son, Francis, born; *Poor Richard's Almanack* first produced.

1736
Francis Franklin dies; Franklin forms America's first fire brigade, the Union Fire Company of Philadelphia.

1740
Publishes his design for a fireplace.

1743
Daughter, Sarah, born; publishes *A Proposal for Promoting Useful Knowledge*.

1744
American Philosophical Society founded.

1746
Sees Doctor Spence's electrical demonstrations in Boston.

1747
Starts his own electrical experiments; forms a voluntary defense association in Philadelphia.

1748
Retires from printing.

1751
"Experiments and Observations on Electricity" communicated to Peter Collinson in London, and published.

1752
"Sentry box" experiment successful in France; Franklin performs experiment with kite in America.

1753
Awarded medal by the Royal Society; becomes deputy postmaster general of North America.

1754
Attends the Albany Congress; urges union of the colonies.

1755
Organizes defense against Indians following the Gnadenhütten massacre.

1756
Elected a fellow of the Royal Society.

1757
Pennsylvania's representative in London.

1762
Returns to Philadelphia; devises the *armonica*.

Slavery was an accepted way of life in colonial America, and almost all of our country's Founding Fathers owned slaves. As he became prosperous due to his printing business, Benjamin Franklin owned two slaves, who worked as personal servants. However, as he grew older, his views on slavery changed. He freed his slaves, and toward the end of his life, he joined an organization that actively worked to end slavery: the Pennsylvania Society for Promoting the Abolition of Slavery. Franklin wrote the letter that appears on the opposite page in 1789, asking that the federal government end slavery and work to educate former slaves so that they could become useful members of American society.

An Address

To the PUBLIC,

from the

Pennsylvania Society for promoting the Abolition of Slavery, and the Relief of Free Negroes, unlawfully held in Bondage.

It is with peculiar satisfaction we assure the friends of humanity, that in prosecuting the design of our association, our endeavours have proved successful, far beyond our most sanguine expectations.

Encouraged by this success, and by the daily progress of that luminous and benign spirit of liberty, which is diffusing itself throughout the world; and humbly hoping for the continuance of the divine blessing on our labors, we have ventured to make an important addition to our original plan, and do therefore, earnestly solicit the support and assistance, of all who can feel the tender emotions of sympathy and compassion, or relish the exalted pleasure of beneficence.

Slavery is such an atrocious debasement of human nature, that its very extirpation, if not performed with solicitous care, may sometimes open a source of serious evils.

The unhappy man who has long been treated as a brute animal, too frequently sinks beneath the common standard of the human species. The galling chains that bind his body, do also fetter his intellectual faculties, and impair the social affections of his heart. Accustomed to move like a mere machine, by the will of a master, reflection is suspended; he has not the power of choice; and reason and conscience, have but little influence over his conduct: because he is chiefly governed by the passion of fear. He is poor and friendless——perhaps worn out by extreme labor, age and disease.

Under such circumstances, freedom may often prove a misfortune to himself, and prejudicial to society.

Attention to emancipated black people, it is therefore to be hoped, will become a branch of our national police; but as far as we contribute to promote this emancipation, so far that attention is evidently a serious duty, incumbent on us, and which we mean to discharge to the best of our judgment and abilities.

To instruct; to advise; to qualify those who have been restored to freedom, for the exercise and enjoyment of civil liberty. To promote in them habits of industry; to furnish them with employments suited to their age, sex, talents, and other circumstances; and to procure their children an education calculated for their future situation in life. These are the great outlines of the annexed plan, which we have adopted, and which we conceive will essentially promote the public good, and the happiness of these our hitherto too much neglected fellow creatures.

A Plan so extensive cannot be carried into execution, without considerable pecuniary resources, beyond the present ordinary funds of the society. We hope much from the generosity of enlightened and benevolent freemen, and will gratefully receive any donations or subscriptions for this purpose, which may be made to our treasurer, James Starr, *or to* James Pemberton, *chairman, of our committee of correspondence.*

Signed by order of the Society,

B. FRANKLIN, *President.*

Philadelphia, 9th of *November*, 1789.

1764

Back in London, again to represent Pennsylvania.

1765

Stamp Act passed by Parliament.

1769

Elected president of the American Philosophical Society.

1773

Boston Tea Party.

1774

Humiliated before the British government by Royal solicitor Alexander Wedderburn in January for his role in supporting the American colonies; relinquishes post of deputy postmaster general; Deborah Franklin dies.

1775

Returns to Philadelphia; American War of Independence breaks out.

1776

Helps to draft the Declaration of Independence; sails to Paris to seek French support in the war.

1778

Thanks in part to Franklin's efforts, France joins the American colonies in their war for independence from Britain.

1781

British forces, commanded by General Cornwallis, surrender to the Americans at Yorktown, ending the major fighting of the Revolution.

1783

A peace treaty officially ending the war is signed in Paris; Franklin observes the world's first balloon flights.

1784
Joins a team of scientists investigating Mesmerism.

1785
Returns to Philadelphia for the last time.

1787
Selected as one of Pennsylvania's delegates to the Constitutional Convention.

1790
Benjamin Franklin dies on April 17.

Further Reading

Brands, H.W. *The First American: The Life and Times of Benjamin Franklin*. New York, Doubleday, 2000.

Isaacson, Walter. *Benjamin Franklin: An American Life*. New York: Simon and Schuster, 2003.

Marcovitz, Hal. *The Declaration of Independence: Forming a New Nation*. Philadelphia: Mason Crest, 2015.

Middlekauff, Robert. *The Glorious Cause: The American Revolution, 1763–1789*. New York: Oxford University Press, 2007.

Morus, Iwan Rhys. *The Oxford Illustrated History of Science*. New York: Oxford University Press, 2017.

Strum, Richard M. *Causes of the American Revolution*. Stockton, NJ: OTTN Publishing, 2005.

Wootton, David. *The Invention of Science: A New History of the Scientific Revolution*. New York: Harper Perennial, 2016.

Statue of Benjamin Franklin outside the old City Hall building in Boston.

Franklin sat for this portrait by the the French artist Jean-Baptiste Greuze in 1777, soon after his arrival in France.

Internet Resources

www.fi.edu/benjamin-franklin/resources

The Franklin Institute is a world-renowned museum of science and technology in Philadelphia. This page on the Institute's website provides links to explore the history of Benjamin Franklin's scientific experiments and legacy.

www.ushistory.org/franklin/fun

Visitors to the Fun With Franklin site can play games, solve puzzles, and conduct scientific experiments, just like Benjamin Franklin did.

www.pbs.org/ktca/liberty

The companion website to the PBS series *Liberty! The American Revolution*.

www.loc.gov/teachers/classroommaterials/ presentationsandactivities/presentations/timeline/amrev/ amrev.html

This guide to the American Revolution includes materials adapted for use in the classroom. It's maintained by the Library of Congress.

www.sciencenewsforstudents.org

Science News for Students is an award-winning online publication dedicated to providing age-appropriate, topical science news to learners, parents and educators.

www.pbs.org/wgbh/nova

The website of NOVA, a science series that airs on PBS. The series produces in-depth science programming on a variety of topics, from the latest technology to the deepest mysteries of the natural world.

Series Glossary of Key Terms

anomaly—something that differs from the expectations generated by an established scientific idea. Anomalous observations may inspire scientists to reconsider, modify, or come up with alternatives to an accepted theory or hypothesis.

evidence—test results and/or observations that may either help support or help refute a scientific idea. In general, raw data are considered evidence only once they have been interpreted in a way that reflects on the accuracy of a scientific idea.

experiment—a scientific test that involves manipulating some factor or factors in a system in order to see how those changes affect the outcome or behavior of the system.

hypothesis—a proposed explanation for a fairly narrow set of phenomena, usually based on prior experience, scientific background knowledge, preliminary observations, and logic.

natural world—all the components of the physical universe, as well as the natural forces at work on those things.

objective—to consider and represent facts without being influenced by biases, opinions, or emotions. Scientists strive to be objective, not subjective, in their reasoning about scientific issues.

observe—to note, record, or attend to a result, occurrence, or phenomenon.

science—knowledge of the natural world, as well as the process through which that knowledge is built through testing ideas with evidence gathered from the natural world.

subjective—referring to something that is influenced by biases, opinions, and/or emotions. Scientists strive to be objective, not subjective, in their reasoning about scientific issues.

test—an observation or experiment that could provide evidence regarding the accuracy of a scientific idea. Testing involves figuring out what one would expect to observe if an idea were correct and comparing that expectation to what one actually observes.

theory—a broad, natural explanation for a wide range of phenomena in science. Theories are concise, coherent, systematic, predictive, and broadly applicable, often integrating and generalizing many hypotheses. Theories accepted by the scientific community are generally strongly supported by many different lines of evidence. However, theories may be modified or overturned as new evidence is discovered.

Statue of Benjamin Franklin outside the old U.S. Post Office building in Washington, D.C.

Index

About the Author

Bradley Sneddon is a graduate of the University of Delaware. He teaches biology in Newark, Delaware, where he lives with his wife and their two dogs. His other books for young people include a biography of Charles Darwin in the SCIENTISTS AND THEIR DISCOVERIES series.

Photo Credits

American Philosophical Society: 13; Connecticut Historical Society: 8; Everett Historical: 16, 30, 37, 52, 58, 68, 70, 75, 83, 88; Vince Flango: 49; Independence Historical National Park: 62, 71, 73, 77; The Library Company of Philadelphia: 32; Library of Congress: 12, 14, 33, 42, 44, 47, 56, 64, 65, 69, 76; Massachusetts Historical Society: 10; National Oceanic and Atmospheric Administration: 57; National Portrait Gallery, London: 1; used under license from Shutterstock, Inc.: 15, 20, 35, 54, 66, 87; darqdesign / shutterstock.com: 92; Diego Grandi / shutterstock.com: 6; George Sheldon / shutterstock.com: 19; Wellcome Library: 22, 24, 27, 28, 39.